RSPCA

ANNUAL 2013

This book belongs to:

Jade

Scholastic Children's Books
Euston House, 24 Eversholt Street,
London, NW1 1DB

Project Manager: Neil Kelly
For Scholastic Ltd: Jill Sawyer, Elizabeth Scoggins
Scholastic Ltd would like to thank all at the RSPCA who helped with content for this Annual

Book Design: Dynamo Design Ltd
www.dynamodesign.co.uk

ISBN: 978 1407 13491 8

© RSPCA 2012

All rights reserved.
Published in the UK by Scholastic Ltd, 2012

Printed and bound by L.E.G.O., Italy

RSPCA name and logo are trade marks of RSPCA used by Scholastic Ltd under license from RSPCA Trading Ltd.

Scholastic Ltd will donate a minimum of 15p to RSPCA Trading Ltd (which pays all its taxable profits to the RSPCA, Registered in England and Wales Charity No. 219099) from every book sold.

CONTENTS

Welcome...	6	Hedgehog Hospital	38
British Wildlife	8	Burrow Race	40
Dogs	10	Which is Your Perfect Pet?	42
Real-life Rescues:		Meet the RSPCA!	44
Quinn the Jack Russell	12	Fundraising for the RSPCA	46
Doggy Doodles	14	Going Underground	48
Fun and Games	16	It's a Vet's Life!	50
Cats	18	Winter and Summer	52
British Garden Birds	20	RSPCA Campaigns	54
Hunting Birds	22	Join the Club!	56
Frogs and Toads	24	Are You an Animal Expert?	58
Fun and Games	26	Puzzle and Quiz Answers	60
Rabbits	28		
Furry Friends	30		
Horses and Ponies	32		
Real-life Rescues:			
Polly the Horse	34		
Animal Antics!	36		

Welcome...

Hi there! Welcome to the RSPCA Annual 2013 – if you love animals, this is the book for you! You'll find out everything you need to know about British wildlife and your favourite pets, from delightful dogs and cute cats to beautiful birds, fascinating foxes and burrowing badgers.

Packed with animal facts, pictures and top tips, there's loads to learn and lots of fun puzzles and quizzes to test your animal knowledge. You'll also read about the RSPCA's real-life rescues of animals in trouble, including our fabulous front-cover puppy, Quinn. Find out about a day in the life of a vet and the different ways the RSPCA works with animals. Discover how your own fundraising efforts could help some of the animals in our care, and get creative with our recipe for making owl-shaped cookies! There's also a competition to enter, with a selection of fantastic RSPCA goodies up for grabs. The first-prize includes an overnight stay at RSPCA Mallydams Wood, our very special wildlife and education centre near Hastings.

We've had a lot of fun putting this annual together, and we really hope you enjoy reading it. So turn the page, and get ready to meet all of our animal-tastic, furry, feathered, slippery and spiky friends!

Enjoy your Annual!

Caring for Animals

RSPCA staff are trained to look after all sorts of animals, from cuddly kittens to spiky hedgehogs. The RSPCA – short for Royal Society for the Prevention of Cruelty to Animals – has many branches throughout the British Isles and its hard-working staff and volunteers are on duty around the clock to look after wild animals and injured or neglected pets.

Family Fun

Every pet deserves to live a happy life, like the dog shown here with his family. Not all pets are so lucky, but the RSPCA does all it can to find caring, responsible new owners for neglected or mistreated animals.

British Wildlife

The British Isles are home to lots of different wild animals, from beautiful birds that soar through the sky to furry, four-legged foragers and stealthy hunters. Many of these animals may need the RSPCA's help when they are injured or get sick, and the organisation's wildlife centres are equipped to deal with everything from a hedgehog with a bad cold to an owl with a broken wing!

Let's take a look at some of the amazing creatures both great and small that can be found in the fields, trees and hedgerows of Britain...

Owl

These large, beautiful birds have small beaks, flat faces, sharp claw-like talons, and very good long-range eyesight. They love eating mice, insects and smaller birds. Some owls also hunt fish, using their talons to snatch prey out of the water. Britain's native owls include the Barn Owl (shown right), as well as the Long-eared, Tawny and Short-eared varieties.

Squirrel

Squirrels belong to a group of animals called rodents. Like all rodents, they have two large teeth in their upper and lower jaws, which are used for gnawing nuts and seeds. Grey squirrels like the one shown below were introduced into Britain from North America over 130 years ago, and they have replaced the native red squirrel in most of the British Isles.

Hare

These fast-moving creatures look a lot like rabbits, but they are usually much larger and have longer ears. They feed on grass, flowers, fruit, vegetables and many types of plants. Hares can run very fast – the European hare can reach a top speed of about 45 mph (72 km/h), nearly twice as fast as the speediest human!

Fox

A member of the canine, or dog, family, foxes will eat almost anything. Foxes live in both rural (countryside) urban (city) areas, and although they are good hunters they prefer to scavenge as it's easier and less tiring! A fox's typical diet includes worms, beetles, berries, carrion (dead animals), mice, rats, rabbits and birds.

Badger

These black-and-white burrowers have small heads, short necks, stocky bodies and short tails. Strong claws enable a badger to dig out its underground burrow, or sett, which it fills with soft bedding materials such as grass, straw, leaves or moss. Badgers love to eat mice, caterpillars, worms, plums, moles and hedgehogs.

Hedgehog

An insect-munching little creature that communicates using grunts, snuffles and squeals, the hedgehog is covered in spiky, protective quills. Found in the hedgerows of Britain, hedgehogs live in underground dens and also eat snails, frogs, mushrooms, melons and berries.

Fact File

Britain's mild, damp climate enables many different animals to thrive who would struggle to survive in warmer or cooler surroundings.

The Red Deer is Britain's largest native animal.

Deer

Deer are found all over the world, except for the continents of Australia and Antarctica. These long-legged plant-eaters are ungulates – animals with two toes on each hoof. They are the only animal species to have bony antlers growing on their heads. There are six deer species living wild in Britain today: Red Deer, Roe Deer, Fallow Deer (shown above), Sika Deer, Reeves's Muntjac and Chinese Water Deer.

Dogs

As the saying goes, dogs are man's best friend. Our loyal, four-legged companions can be pets and working animals, and they've been helping out humans for at least 15,000 years! There are hundreds of different breeds, and it's thought that there are about 400 million dogs in the world today.

Dog Facts

- Dogs come in lots of different shapes and sizes, from huge Irish Wolfhounds and Great Danes to tiny Chihuahuas and Terriers.

- At certain frequencies, dogs can detect sounds up to four times quieter than humans can hear.

- The fastest recorded speed for a greyhound dog is 42 mph (67 km/h) – nearly as fast as a mounted racehorse!

- Dogs use special signals to show they want to play. When inviting others to play, a dog crouches on its forelimbs, remains standing on its hindlimbs and may wag its tail or bark. This behaviour is called the 'play bow'.

This Border Collie puppy will grow up to be a helpful, hard-working sheepdog.

Springer Spaniels are fun-loving, excitable dogs. They love people and are ideal family pets.

Yorkshire Terriers are small, friendly dogs that make great companions.

Retrievers were first bred as gun dogs, used to retrieve birds and other prey for hunters.

Boxers are very energetic dogs that love playing with children. They need a lot of exercise!

German Shepherds are a large, powerful breed. They are very good guard dogs.

Loveable Labradors
Labradors are loyal, intelligent and placid animals. They are often trained to work as 'seeing eye' guide dogs for blind people.

Border Collie

Real-life Rescues

Some dogs don't have the best start in life. Our cover-star, Quinn, was one of a number of Jack Russell puppies that weren't being looked after properly by their owner. The RSPCA decided to get the puppies fostered by caring people who could train them and prepare them for rehoming – life in the big, wide world with a new owner.

Quinn is a friendly little dog who makes everyone who meets him smile. He was taken in by his foster carer, an RSPCA worker named Melissa, at the age of 12 weeks. Although he took a while to house train – he was scared of going out into the garden in the rain as a puppy – he's now a confident, loveable dog. He also has a special playmate in the shape of Poppy – Melissa's young cat! They play together and sit by the window watching the world go by. Melissa has now adopted Quinn permanently and he has become a much-loved member of her family. For Quinn, life is woof-tastic!

All about Quinn...

5 things Quinn loves...

- Melissa – he thinks she's the best owner a dog could have!
- Poppy the cat. They're best friends and have loads of fun together.
- Long walks with his doggy friends at RSPCA Headquarters – Bennie, Dougal, Inca, Yogi, Sollie and Stanley.
- His toys, especially his chews, squeaky ducks and stuffed meerkat.
- Playtime in the woods.

5 things Quinn dislikes...

- Bathtime – Quinn doesn't like his fur getting soapy!
- Being towel dried when he's wet.
- Inconsiderate dog owners – his first owner didn't look after Quinn or the other puppies very well.
- Going to see the vet – Quinn gets a bit scared though he knows he's being silly.
- Being treated for fleas.

Here's a very special letter to all our readers from Quinn...

Melissa, Quinn and Poppy's House
The Countryside
(Near the woods)
Oxfordshire
England

Summertime, 2012

Dear RSPCA Annual readers,

Hi, it's Quinn here! I hope you all enjoyed reading about me, and I also really wanted to say a big woof-woof to everybody at the RSPCA to thank them all for finding me such a fantastic new home and owner!

I'm having a great time living with Melissa – we're always going out on long walks in the woods, and I get to spend lots of time with her as she takes me into work at the RSPCA Headquarters every day. One day a week I go to a special crèche – a type of dog nursery – where I play with about 12 other friendly dogs all day long. It's great fun, but very tiring, and when I get home I usually fall fast asleep in my basket!

Best of all is my special friend Poppy. Although lots of dogs don't get on with cats, we're the best of friends and always have lots of fun playing together. I also love Melissa's grandparents as they are very kind to me and give me lots of attention (don't tell Melissa though because she'll think that they're spoiling me).

I know I'm very lucky to have such a great owner and not every dog gets this opportunity – a lot of my friends are still living at RSPCA animal centres, waiting for a new home. Hopefully, one day they'll have a lovely life like me!

I've got to go now as Poppy says that there's a fox in the garden and she wants to sit with me at the window and watch what he's up to. The fox is a regular visitor and comes by every night looking for food. I'm glad I have dog food and a nice warm basket to sleep in – I wouldn't like having to hunt for dinner and sleep outside like he does!

Big barks and happy woof-woofs,

Doggy Doodles

Draw your own Dog!

Grab a fresh sheet of paper and follow these simple steps to learn how to draw man's best friend. It's not as hard as you might think!

All you need is a soft drawing pencil – a B pencil is perfect – together with an eraser and a black pen. So what are you waiting for? Get drawing!

1

To start, draw three simple circles. You need one large one for your dog's chest and two slightly smaller circles – one for its head and one for its behind. Try to position them as they are shown here.

Drawing tip:
Plan ahead. Think carefully about where you are starting your drawing. If you position your circles too low on your piece of paper, you might run out of space for the legs.

2

Now you need to work out the rough shape of your dog. Do this by connecting the circles with two lines for the neck, and two lines for the body. Then add a box shape on the left where your dog's face will be. Lastly, add guide lines to show where you want to draw the tail and the legs – remember to copy the bends of the legs as they are shown here.

Drawing tip:
Look at how long the guide lines for the dog's legs are on the left – they're similar to the width of the body, so be careful not to make yours too long.

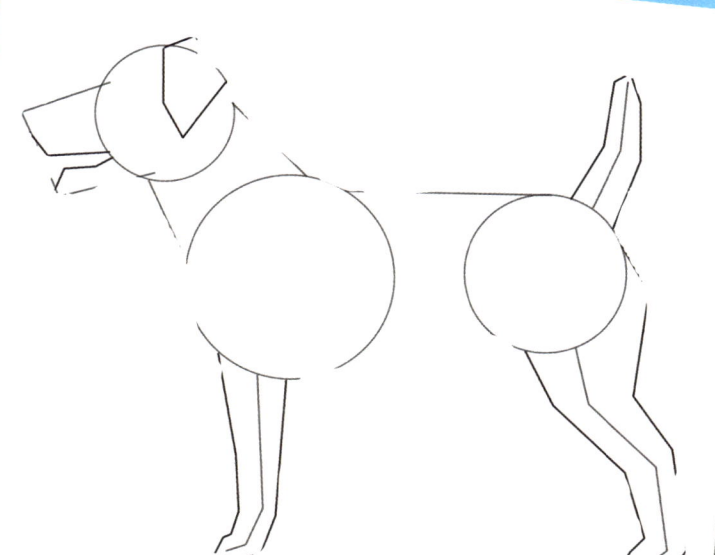

3

Next you can start 'fleshing out' your dog to give it a more life-like look.

Lightly draw simple, straight lines to shape your dog's jaw, legs and tail. If you make any mistakes, you can easily rub them out and give it another go. Don't forget to add an ear!

4

Now your dog is really starting to take shape, but to make it look really realistic, you need to add detail to the face and body. Lightly sketch in an eye, a nose and the extra detail to shape the face, legs, body and tail. Try to copy the shape shown here as closely as you can. Remember to add extra lines for the legs on your dog's far side and to give the paws claws, as shown here.

Drawing tip:
If you leave a small area of the nose and eye white, the paper will make it look as though there is light shining off them.

5

Lastly, take your black pen and go over your outline to finish. Keep the line smooth except where you want to show areas of fluffy fur. If you like, you could also use some coloured pencils to add patches and colour in your dog's tongue – it will really add character!

Fun and Games

Give your brain a workout with these animal-tastic word puzzles...

```
F R O G H J T L M N R O B R E T S M A H
H K Q W B X N Q T Z E T D W L P K L N X
D L N E T T I K R A D S X D O G W Q P L
E U X Y Q R T G A V K L A G B E F N J C
J Z L E B S N O H L I S Y Y L F Q E L A
G E R B I L O Y E N T B K C Q A J S R T
S Q E W D A B N D J E Q H X R L K U G P
H N R C S X Z M G H V M J O L U I O H L
K J T B T F C Q E S C E L S R Z J M J Z
I L N R C O S L H Q B X H U Z S Q N F C
N N E Q Z X Z Y O R D A B Q T L E Y L O
G Z C G F P N V G Y N C D L X F H Q F U
F Q L X R A T L V L O Z A G D W T O A D
I B A R O K B Y T A Y F J L E B W K V J
S Y M S N R A B B I T Q C V S R V H X M
H T I N Q C F H L J W X K B E B G A J O
E B N Y A L N V Y N O P A A A S W R F L
R K A Z C O W Q V D J W X T L E M E N E
A P R Y N G U I N E A P I G K L K X Z Y
```

SEARCH IT!

Can you find the animal words below in the grid above?

ANIMAL CENTRE	DOG	GUINEA PIG	KINGFISHER	RABBIT
BADGER	FLY	HAMSTER	KITTEN	RAT
BAT	FOX	HARE	MOLE	RED KITE
CAT	FROG	HEDGEHOG	MOUSE	SEAL
COW	GERBIL	HORSE	PONY	TOAD

Cats

Cats are one of the most popular pets in Britain, with over eight million of them purring away on our sofas or prowling through our backgardens. They may be smaller and more cuddly than a tiger or a lion, but, like their big cousins, they're still wild at heart!

Cat facts

- Domestic (house) cats are thought to have originated from a type of African Wildcat.
- Cats have powerful, tightly controlled muscles and fast reflexes that allow them to move quickly and gracefully.
- Domestic cats sleep for 12–18 hours a day!
- Cats use a variety of sounds to communicate, including purrs, 'meows', trills, chirrups, growls, yowls and hisses.
- Cats can see better than humans in dark and dim light. They can also detect higher frequencies of sound than dogs or humans.

Like all cats, this ginger tom enjoys spending a lot of his time asleep in a cosy, warm place!

Cats come in lots of colours. This little kitten has white and ginger fur with black stripes.

Kittens are born with their eyes closed. They open them after 7–10 days.

Sensitive whiskers help a cat to judge if it can squeeze and twist its way through narrow spaces.

There are usually 3–4 kittens per litter. They spend most of their waking time playing!

Cats are natural explorers and love to roam around outdoors like their big cat cousins.

Tortoiseshell in trouble
The RSPCA often has to find new homes for cats that have been neglected or abandoned, like this beautiful tortoiseshell.

Tabby Cat

British Garden Birds

Birds are popular visitors in British gardens, brightening up our backyards with their cheery chirping and tuneful warbling! With their attractive, often brightly coloured appearance, it's always fascinating to watch these feathered visitors. Providing food and water is a great way to encourage many different types of birds to visit your garden, especially during the colder months. Be sure to have a go at making our bird-treat recipe – it's packed with everything a bird needs to stay healthy.

Read on for the low-down on the most common birds you're likely to find in a British garden. From the chirpy sparrow to the beautiful blue tit, these bird-brained beauties are all winged wonders...

Thrush

A plump, grey or brown bird with a speckled chest, the thrush loves to eat berries, insects, fruit, worms and snails. The Song Thrush, shown here, is famed for its beautiful, musical song. Thrushes lay speckled eggs in cup-shaped nests that they line with mud.

Finch

Finches usually live in wooded areas, but sometimes they can be found on mountains or even in deserts. There are many types of finch, most of which are different shades of brown, green or black. The Goldfinch shown below has a bright face and yellow wing patch, and it has a twittering song and call. Its long beak helps it to dig out hard-to-reach seeds and insects. In winter, many British goldfinches fly south to warmer areas – some even reach as far as Spain.

Blackbird

One of the most familiar British garden birds, the adult male blackbird has black feathers and a bright orange-yellow beak and eye-ring. The females do not have black plumage – instead, they are brown, often with a spotted or streaked breast. Like the finch and the thrush the blackbird also has a tuneful, pleasant song. Blackbirds are found in many areas, from gardens and the countryside to coasts to hilly areas.

Blue Tit

This beautiful bird, with its distinctive blue, yellow, white and green plumage, is very also very agile. Blue Tits are skilled at hanging upside down from tree branches when searching for food. Their favourite snacks are spiders and insects.

Robin

The most famous British garden bird, especially at Christmas, the Robin's bright-red breast marks it out from other small birds. Males and females look identical, but young birds don't have a red breast – instead they have golden-brown spots. Robins may be pretty, but they are also very territorial and can be aggressive, driving away intruders or rivals.

Sparrow

Lively and noisy with a familiar chirping call, sparrows are found in most parts of the world. Some sparrows scavenge for food in and around cities, and will eat almost anything! The House Sparrow (shown left) mainly eats seeds and weeds. It lives in cities, towns and the countryside, but stays away from woods, grasslands, and deserts.

What seed to feed?

There are different types of seed mixes for birdfeeders, birdtables and ground feeding so decide first which method of feeding birds suits your own garden. The better seed mixtures contain plenty of flaked maize, sunflower seeds, and peanut granules. Birds will eat different things seasonally so adding extra fat or peanuts in the winter will keep the birds well fed. You could also hang out a bird treat – we have a recipe for making one on page 52!

Different seeds attract different birds. Small seeds, such as millet, attract mostly house sparrows, dunnocks, finches, reed buntings and collared doves, while flaked maize is taken readily by blackbirds. Tits and greenfinches favour peanuts and sunflower seeds. Mixes that contain chunks or whole nuts are suitable for winter feeding only. Wheat and barley grains are often included in seed mixtures, but they are really only suitable for pigeons, doves and pheasants, which feed on the ground and tend to scare off smaller birds.

Hunting Birds

Britain is home to many magnificent hunting birds, also known as birds of prey. Using their super-sharp vision to spy food, they mainly hunt small animals while on the wing, including other birds. They have large beaks and powerful talons to help them catch their prey.

The Red Kite belongs to a family of birds that includes eagles, buzzards and harriers. It has angled wings and a forked tail that help it swoop down from the sky to snatch prey such as mice, voles and rabbits. The Red Kite nearly became extinct due to hunting and poisoning, but it has been saved by a protection programme and was successfully re-introduced to the wild in England and Scotland.

Owls are nocturnal hunters, which means that they look for food at night. They rely on stealth to take their prey – their plumage helps them to blend into their surroundings as they silently glide through the night air. Then, in a blur of feathers, they strike!

Red Kite Facts

- Hunting birds like the Red Kite are called 'raptors', from a Latin word meaning to take by force.
- The Red Kite makes its nest high up in a tree, using dead twigs. It lines the nest with grass and sheep's wool.
- To avoid being eaten by an animal such as a fox, a Red Kite will play dead until the danger has passed!
- As well as feeding on living creatures, Red Kites also like to tuck into dead sheep carcasses, with a side order of earthworms. Nice!
- A pair of Red Kites will stay together for life. When they are courting, the birds fly towards each other then turn away at the last moment, touching talons as they pass.

Little Owl

The Little Owl is the smallest owl found in Britain. It can often be seen during the day, resting on high posts or telegraph poles, as well as the roofs of farm buildings. It has at least eight different high-pitched calls.

Barn Owl

The beautiful Barn Owl can be found nesting in farm buildings, haystacks and tree hollows. It's also known as a 'screech owl' because of its hissing, high-pitched call. Long wings help it to glide smoothly through the air.

Owl Facts

- When the Little Owl feels threatened, it wiggles from side to side.
- A Barn Owl's right ear opening is usually large and higher than the one on the left. This helps the owl to pinpoint the location of its prey using its hearing alone.
- The cry of a Tawny Owl is the most well-known of all owl calls, making the distinctive "tu-whit, tu-whoo" sound.

Tawny Owl

The Tawny Owl has rounded wings that allow it to fly with fewer wingbeats and at a greater height than many other owls. It is the most commonly found owl in the British Isles.

Frogs and Toads

Frogs and toads are amphibians – animals that live both on land and in water. They both start off life as fish-like tadpoles with tails for swimming and gills for breathing underwater. The tadpole soon becomes a froglet or toadlet, growing legs and developing lungs for breathing air on land. The tail shrinks, the eyes and mouth get bigger and before long the amphibian is a fully grown frog or toad!

Toads are closely related to frogs but there are a few differences. A toad has rough warty skin, while the frog's skin is smooth. They also tend to be a shade of brown, green or grey in colour whereas frogs are usually shades of green, yellow or brown.

A common toad, taking it easy on a Fly Agaric toadstool in Britain's Peak District.

A Frog's Life Cycle

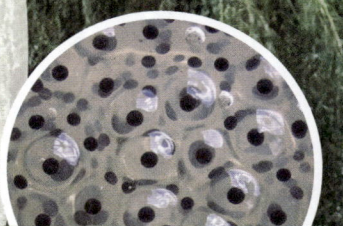

1. The female frog lays thousands of jelly-covered eggs, called frogspawn.

2. Inside the jelly, the dot-like egg grows into a tiny creature called a tadpole.

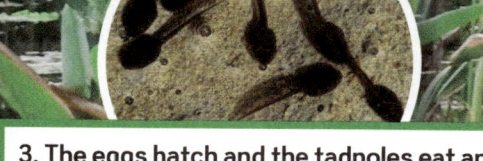

3. The eggs hatch and the tadpoles eat and grow. They use their tail to swim around.

4. The tadpole is now a froglet – it has legs and lungs so it can breathe on land.

5. A fully grown frog, ready to leap onto a lily pad or plunge into a pond!

The White's Tree Frog can protect itself by changing colour to blend into its surroundings. This frog is native to Australia and New Guinea, but many people in Britain keep them as pets.

The male Natterjack Toad is one of Britain's noisiest animals! It has a vocal sac under its chin that fills up with air and amplifies its mating call, which can be heard several kilometres away.

Frog and Toad Facts

- Frogs have long, powerful hind legs for jumping and webbed toes to help them swim.

- A toad's long, sticky tongue helps it to catch insects, slugs and small worms.

- Toads release a substance from their skin that tastes disgusting to creatures who try eat to them. Yuck!

- There are approximately 2,000 eggs in a typical clump of frog spawn.

- Toads do not jump like frogs – instead they crawl and hop.

- Frogs can breathe through their skin as well as their mouths.

- Frogs lay their eggs in clumps, while toads lay their eggs in long, stretched-out chains.

Save our Frogs!

The common British frog is becoming more rare because of the destruction of its natural living areas, or habitats. Ponds have been filled in, and hedges and ditches have been removed. Also the use of poisons to kill insects has meant that food is harder to find. People can help by building a pond in their back garden. This will attract amphibians and provide a place for them to lay spawn.

Fun and Games

Here are some more animal puzzles plus a fun quiz to test your brain. Are you up to the challenge?

The answers can be found on pages 60-61!

What Kind of Animal are You?

Ever wondered what type of animal you most resemble? Try our quiz to find out – don't worry though, it won't bite!

1 What are your favourite foods?
a) I like eating everything!
b) Fish
c) Vegetables
d) Meat

2 What are your relationships like with your family?
a) We're very competitive
b) My family's OK, but I like my own company the best
c) We get on well but sometimes we fight
d) I love being with my family more than anything

3 Where do you spend most time?
a) Outdoors
b) Inside, in the warm
c) Indoors and outdoors, depending on the time of year
d) I spend my time with my friends and family, wherever they are

4 Which of the following best describes your personality?
a) I like to do my own thing – I don't follow the crowd
b) I'm a bit bossy and like to be in charge
c) I like to follow others rather than being the leader
d) I'm loyal and I like being with people

5 What is your favourite outdoor place?
a) Woodlands and countryside
b) Gardens, hedges and trees
c) Grassy fields and meadows
d) Parks, big open spaces and the seaside

6 Home is:
a) A quiet, safe place
b) A warm place where I eat, sleep and get lots of attention
c) Somewhere where I'm fed well and looked after
d) Where the heart is, with my family

7 Which of the following activities do you enjoy most?
a) Hiding
b) Sleeping
c) Eating
d) Running

8 When you eat do you like to:
a) Eat some food now and hide the rest to eat tomorrow
b) Eat your own food quickly
c) Eat as you go and carry on 'grazing' all day
d) Eat your own food and try to grab food belonging to others

9 Which of the following best describes your personality?
a) Cunning and clever
b) Independent and resourceful
c) Quiet and shy
d) Playful and friendly

10 Which best describes your physical abilities?
a) Good hearing and eyesight
b) Agile and flexible
c) Quick reflexes and good at jumping
d) A good swimmer

Odd One Out...

Which of these four cute boxer puppies is the odd one out?

Spot the Difference

Take a really close look at the two pictures below. There are six differences between them – can you spot them all?

Rabbits

Rabbits are big-eared, plant-eating animals that are probably the cuddliest pet you can have! They have super-soft fur and are very friendly, but they need to be looked after carefully as they can get scared easily. Most pet rabbits live in a hutch outdoors, but some are house-trained and live indoors. Very clever bunnies can even learn to come when called, like dogs!

Rabbit Facts

- Rabbits have powerful hindlegs that allow them to reach speeds of up to 50 mph (80 km/h) for short bursts.
- Wild rabbits dig lots of connecting tunnels called 'warrens' that can cover more than two acres of land!
- Warrens can house 50 or more rabbits!
- Pet rabbits can be taught to respond to their owner's commands using reward-based training. They can also be house-trained.
- A rabbit's top front teeth are called 'incisors' and grow at a rate of 3 mm a week! Eating lots of grass and hay helps to wear a rabbit's teeth down.

A rabbit loves to be cuddled – just be gentle, so that it doesn't feel stressed or scared.

A good sense of smell and super-sensitive hearing warns rabbits when danger is coming.

Our big-eared friends can run very quickly if they are frightened or startled.

Hold your rabbit carefully, supporting it from beneath, so that it feels safe.

Rabbits love carrots, but give them as a treat. Your pet should eat grass, hay and leafy plants.

Rabbits need lots of exercise, access to a secure exercise area and a safe place to sleep.

Wrapped-up rabbit
When you take your rabbit for a check-up, the vet may carefully wrap it in a towel to keep it calm while he or she gently examines your pet.

Rabbit

Furry Friends

If you don't have much space at home to look after a larger animal like a dog, cat or rabbit, one of these small furry pets might be just the thing for you.

Guinea pigs, gerbils, mice and hamsters are all small, furry rodents. Each one needs to be looked after differently, so read on to discover more about each animal.

Guinea Pig

These squeaky, chatty little animals can be kept in an indoor or outdoor hutch with a large exercise area. They need company so it is best to keep them in neutered pairs from the same litter.

Guinea pigs need a quiet space, away from draughts and direct sunlight, that isn't too hot or too cold. They should have enough space to run around and room to stand up on their back legs. They also need bedding, such as soft dust-free hay to help them stay warm, and something to shelter in when they are frightened. Pipes and a tunnel are ideal for this.

If you give a guinea pig gentle attention from an early age they will learn to trust you and see you as a friend.

Guinea pigs need grooming a couple of times a week, but long-haired guinea pigs need grooming every day. A special grooming brush from the pet shop can be used, but a baby brush works just as well.

Guinea pigs come in a wide variety of colours and love to be with guinea pig friends.

Gerbil

These little creatures love to burrow. A 'gerbilarium' is just right for them to live in – this is a tank that is filled with safe digging material, such as compost, with a cage on top for them to play in. They'll also need a nest box where they can snooze during the day – away from loud noises and busy areas is best.

Hamster

There are several breeds of hamster, in various sizes. The Syrian hamster is a good choice as it is a larger breed and may be easier to handle. When you bring your hamster home, be quiet and gentle with it. It should be picked up by cupping it with two hands and then opening the hands so that the hamster is sitting on joint palms. Handle it as often as you can, but not when it is sleeping or resting.

Mice

Mice are social animals that like each others' company! A mouse cage should have enough room for them to nest in and plenty of cardboard tubes, tunnels and shelters for them to hide out in. You should check their water bottles every day to make sure they aren't blocked with nesting materials.

RSPCA: TOP TIP!

You'll need an adult to help you trim your pet's claws regularly, but you should also take your rodent to the vet. A vet will check your pet's claws and make sure their teeth are healthy, too.

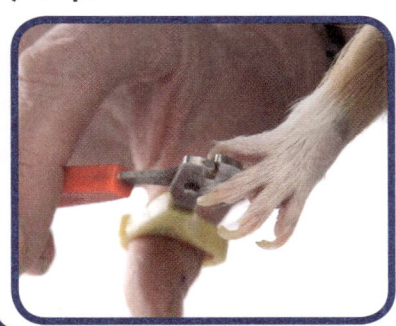 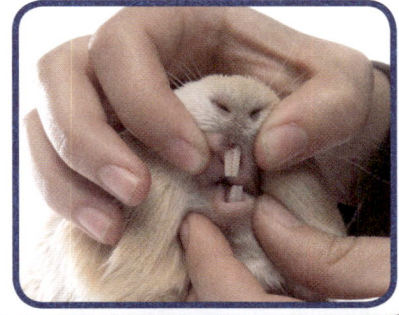

Rodent Facts

- Another name for a guinea pig is a cavy.
- Hamsters are known for their large cheek pouches, which they use to store food to eat later.
- A baby mouse can be called a pinky or a kitten.
- Gerbils thump their feet if they are frightened or startled.

31

Horses and Ponies

Horses need a lot of care and attention and can be fun to ride if they get a lot of patient and gentle training. They come in many shapes and sizes. A pony is a small horse – in fact, some fully grown ponies are the same size as the foals of larger horse breeds. Looking after a horse is hard work!

If you'd like to try horse-riding, there are lots of places in Britain where you can take an introductory lesson.

Horse Facts

- Horses and ponies are social animals – they like to be around other horses and shouldn't be kept by themselves. They enjoy visits from humans, too.
- Stables must be 'mucked out' daily – that means cleaning up all the poo!
- Horse and ponies need a lot of water to drink and hay or grass to eat. They spend 16 to 18 hours a day grazing.
- Horses need lots of exercise – they should be let out to run around or go for a ride every day.
- Grooming is essential – a horse or pony should be brushed all over and have its hooves checked daily.
- Horses and ponies wear special U-shaped metal shoes that must be fitted by a specialist known as a farrier.

A calm, gentle pony is an ideal choice for a small child when they are learning to ride.

Some horses take part in competitions such as dressage and eventing.

Horses can become affectionate to their owners if they are treated kindly and gently.

Foals stay close to their mothers for 4–6 months before spending more time apart.

Horses and ponies carry people and heavy loads in all areas from busy cities to snowy hilltops.

Ponies come in many breeds and sizes, from tiny 'miniature' ponies to larger animals.

Making friends
Many horses are friendly, but be careful how you approach them. Talk to them and don't try to 'sneak up' on them from behind as they may sense danger and strike out with their hooves.

Shetland Ponies

Real-life Rescues

When the RSPCA was called in to help Polly the horse, things didn't look good for the exhausted, starving three-year-old skewbald. Poor Polly had collapsed in a field in East Yorkshire, weighing only 264 kilograms – half what her weight should be. She was taken to RSPCA Felledge Equine and Animal Centre near Durham, where the vet put her on a special diet. It took six months for Polly to reach her normal weight, get healthy and begin to trust humans again. The RSPCA also had to find out if she could be trained to be ridden, which would make it easier to find a new owner.

Polly's groom, Rachael, worked with Polly to build up her confidence. In time, Polly was happy to wear a bridle and saddle. She also learnt to stand at a gate, tackle obstacle courses and walk past scary objects she hadn't seen before. Eventually the time was right for Polly to go to a new home. The happy horse settled in straight away. Her new owner, Krissy, said "When we hack out Polly thinks everyone in the street is there to say hello to her! She is pure love – there's no other way to describe her."

All about Polly...

3 things Polly loves...

- Krissy, her new owner. She takes great care of Polly and they always have fun hacking, cantering and galloping!
- Eating lots of grass and hay – Polly loves her food!
- Rachael and everyone at RSPCA Felledge for all that they did to get Polly well again and ready for a new home.

3 things Polly dislikes..

- Horse owners who don't look after their animals.
- Being tired, thirsty and starving hungry.
- Itchy skin lice and nasty worms that upset her tummy. Polly had both of these when the RSPCA took her in, but they soon got rid of them.

Polly with her RSPCA groom, Rachael.

Polly with Krissy, her new owner.

Polly would like to say hello to you all...

The Stables
Near Krissy's house
Not far from RSPCA Felledge
County Durham
England
Summertime, 2012

Dear RSPCA Annual readers,

Hello everyone! I just thought I'd say hi and let you all know how I'm getting on at my new home. As you'll know from my story, life was pretty bad a while back. I was really ill because my old owner hadn't fed or groomed me properly for ages. Luckily for me a member of the public found me and called in the RSPCA. A kind inspector named Sally got me into RSPCA Felledge and soon I was on the mend!

It took quite a while for me to enjoy being around people again, and I really wasn't sure if I was happy with the idea of having a rider. My amazing groom, Rachael, helped me get over my worries! She was very kind and gentle, and she used a special technique to help me. She would walk behind me, holding the reins and pulling on them when she wanted me to stop, turn and move forward.

I got a lot more confident and before long, Rachael put a saddle and bridle on me and we went for our very first ride together! I really enjoyed it, and I soon learned how to trot and canter.

It was difficult saying goodbye to Rachael and everyone at RSPCA Felledge, but when Krissy came along I knew we were going to get on really well. She really looks after me – my stable is warm and dry and there's always loads of food to eat. I fitted in really quickly to my new home, in fact Krissy says it's like I've been here forever! At the moment we're working on building up my stamina with lots of long-distance runs, so I get plenty of exercise and fresh air – life is really good now! Krissy gives me lots of attention too – she always knows how to cheer me up if I'm feeling a bit sad!

The great thing is that Krissy lives quite near RSPCA Felledge, so I can go and see Rachael and my old friends there to catch up on the latest news – in fact, you could say that they're our neigh-bours (that's a little horse joke – well, I think it's funny!)

Happy hacking!

Polly x

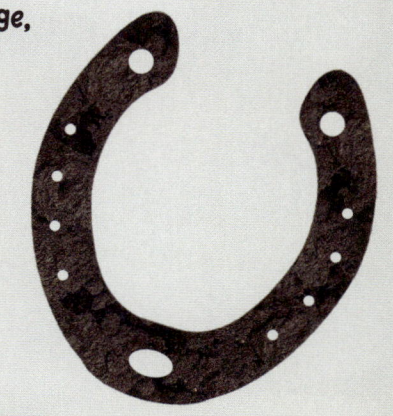

35

Animal Antics!

Life is full of funny moments whenever animals are around! They could be playing, up to something silly – or even just looking adorable. These animal-tastic snaps capture just a few brilliant moments with pets and wildlife alike.

Why not try taking some cute and funny photos of your own pets and thinking of some captions? You'll have to be quick though – if you blink, you'll miss them!

We love playing leap-fox!

All this for some hay!

Anyone seen my hat?

These water taxis are busy today!

Hedgehog Hospital

The RSPCA's West Hatch Wildlife and Animal Centre near Taunton in Somerset looks after lots of animals, including around 280 hedgehogs a year. In late autumn and winter many hedgehogs are brought in with lawn mower or strimmer injuries – the spiky animals shelter in gardens and can often be injured.

Winter – when food is scarce – can be a difficult time. Hedgehogs need to eat a lot to lay down enough fat to use as a food supply while they sleep, or hibernate, through the cold months. These little animals are often brought into the centre, where the wildlife assistants feed them up before eventually releasing them back into the wild.

When handling a hedgehog, RSPCA staff always wear gloves for hygiene purposes.

Caring for hedgehogs at West Hatch...

Injured hedgehogs are often very dehydrated so the vet will give them a milk substitute using a dropper.

These three baby hedgehogs are tucking into a nourishing meal of oats and milk substitute.

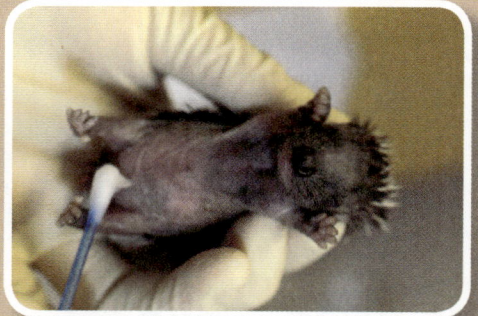

Using a cotton bud is a good way of removing dirt and debris to clean up a grubby hedgehog!

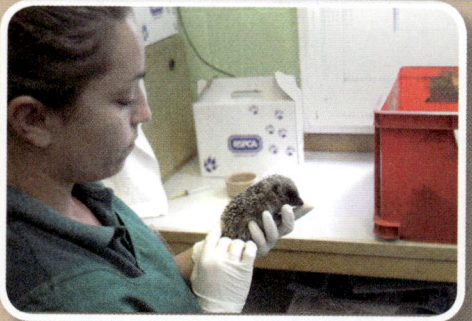

Here the wildlife assistant uses tweezers to remove debris stuck between the animal's spines.

This little hedgehog curls up into a ball as his weight is checked by the wildlife assistant.

This fully recovered, healthy hedgehog is ready to be released back into the wild.

Hedgehog Facts

- A hedgehog has about 7,000 spines covering its back and sides. When it feels threatened, it curls up into a spiky ball for protection.
- Its favourite foods are beetles, caterpillars, earthworms, slugs and snails. Yuck!
- A baby hedgehog is called a hoglet.
- Hedgehogs sleep through the winter in nests called 'hibernacula'. They build these under timber buildings, in piles of leaves and brushwood or in hedgerows.
- Never give a hedgehog milk as this can cause a stomach upset. Give it water to drink and minced meat, fresh liver, chopped boiled eggs or hedgehog food.

Did you know?

A single hedgehog can keep an average garden free of pests by eating up to 200 grams of insects each night!

Burrow Race

In the autumn, many wild animals are building up their food stores and getting ready for winter. Why not see if you can help them by playing our Burrow Race game? Grab a dice and some playing pieces (or small coins if you don't have any). Place all the pieces on the first space to begin. The first player to the Winter Burrow wins!

START HERE!

- Roll a 6 to start the game. Roll again to take your turn.
- It's a sunny day – run on 2 spaces.
- The weather is too bad to forage. Wait here for a turn.
- Fallen apples! Gather them and move forward a space.
- Quick! There's a shortcut to some more food here.
- Another animal has found your food store. Start again.
- You need bedding to keep warm. Go back 3 spaces.
- A friend has given you food – take another turn.
- Rain! Collect the worms and move forward a space.
- Oh, no a flood! Wait a turn to dig a new food store.

THE WINTER BURROW

- You've found lots of nuts. Move forward 2 spaces.
- It's snowing. Miss a turn while you shelter.
- You haven't collected enough food. Go back 3 spaces.
- YOU WIN!
- Winter is nearly here! Hurry forward 3 spaces.

Animal Sudoku

Here are some Sudoku-style number puzzles to test your brain! In puzzle A, complete each row, column and group of four squares, so that the numbers 1 to 4 appear only once.
Puzzle B is a bit trickier – fill in each row, each column and each smaller group of nine squares, so that the numbers 1 to 9 appear only once. The answers for both puzzles are on page 62. Good luck!

A

	4		1
		3	2
2			
		2	4

B

	3		5		7	2	6	8
6	7	2	3	8				1
1	5	8	9	6		7	3	4
		5	2	4	8	6	1	
8		1			5	9	4	2
4	2	7	6	9		3		
5	1		8	2			7	3
2	8	6		7	3		5	9
7		3	1	5	9		2	6

41

Which is Your Perfect Pet?

Getting a pet is a big commitment. They can be expensive and require a lot of care and attention. You also need to be sure you have enough space at home if you want a larger animal. Be sure that you make just the right choice for you!

Use this fun chart to help you decide which animal would be the perfect pet to suit your personality – a puppy, a kitten, a rabbit or a hamster?

START HERE!

At the weekend, you are most likely to be …

C → … at the local park, running around, playing on the swings – anything – so long as you don't have to sit still.

B → … helping out around the house, finishing off school projects or pursuing your hobbies, but always super-busy.

A → … reading a good book somewhere quiet so no one will interrupt you.

Your teacher has given you maths homework – when you get home, do you tackle it straightaway?

NO → It's the holidays! If you could, would you sleep all day long?

YES → After school, you would rather …

A → … spend time relaxing and having fun with your closest friends.

B → On a hot day, you would rather …

In your lunch break, do you always play outside?

YES → If you were bored, would you be more likely to …
- **A**
- **B**

NO → On a hot day, you would rather …

YES / **NO**

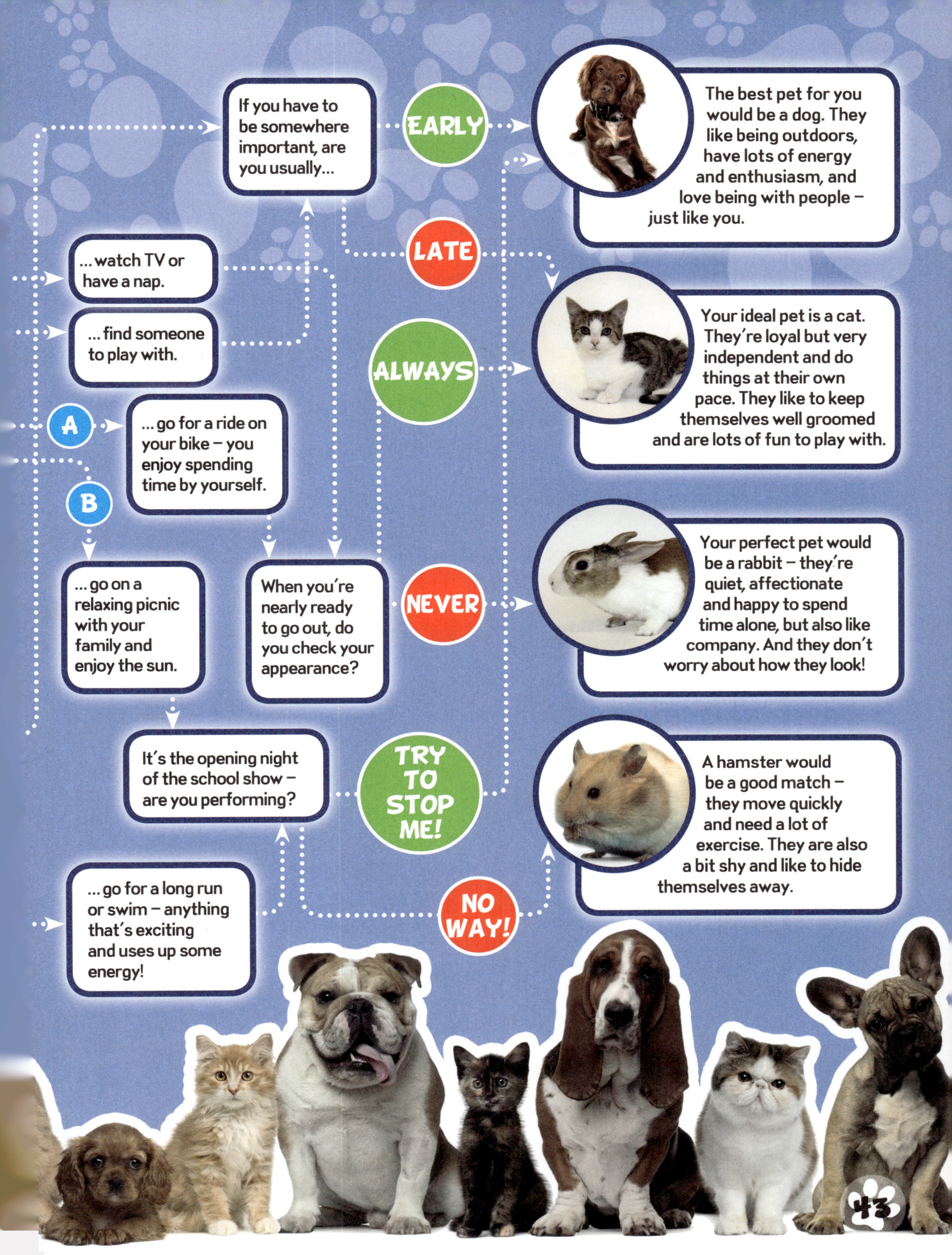

If you have to be somewhere important, are you usually...

- **EARLY** → The best pet for you would be a dog. They like being outdoors, have lots of energy and enthusiasm, and love being with people – just like you.

- **LATE** → ...watch TV or have a nap. / ...find someone to play with.

When you're nearly ready to go out, do you check your appearance?

- **ALWAYS** → Your ideal pet is a cat. They're loyal but very independent and do things at their own pace. They like to keep themselves well groomed and are lots of fun to play with.

- **NEVER** → Your perfect pet would be a rabbit – they're quiet, affectionate and happy to spend time alone, but also like company. And they don't worry about how they look!

A ...go for a ride on your bike – you enjoy spending time by yourself.

B ...go on a relaxing picnic with your family and enjoy the sun.

It's the opening night of the school show – are you performing?

- **TRY TO STOP ME!** → A hamster would be a good match – they move quickly and need a lot of exercise. They are also a bit shy and like to hide themselves away.

- **NO WAY!**

...go for a long run or swim – anything that's exciting and uses up some energy!

RSPCA Competition

Would you like to see for yourself exactly how the RSPCA helps Britain's amazing animals? Well, now's your chance with our fantastic competition! The lucky winner plus family and friends – up to a total of 6 people – will be invited to an overnight stay at RSPCA Mallydams Wood, near Hastings.

You'll get an exclusive tour of the wildlife centre, as well as the education centre and the woodland nature reserve. There will be lots of fun, organised activities, where you'll meet RSPCA staff and learn about their work. You'll also get the chance to spend time with the many different animals in their care, from badgers and owls to dormice, foxes and seals!

As a bonus, the lucky winner will receive an RSPCA goodie bag, which includes plush soft animal toys as well as an RSPCA lunchbox and flask. If you missed out on the top prize but are one of the 25 runners-up, you'll also receive one of these animal-tastic goodie bags!

Mallydams Facts

- RSPCA Mallydams Wood has treated over 35,000 sick, injured and orphaned wild animals since it opened it 1951. It is surrounded by 55 acres of woodland, with nearby farms and beaches.
- Over 433 different animal species have been recorded living in or visiting the wood.
- A local artist named Horace Quick (1891–1966) gave Mallydams Wood to the RSPCA in 1961, so that the woodland could be used to help preserve British wildlife.

1st Prize: Overnight stay and exclusive tour of RSPCA Mallydams Wood, plus goodie bag

25 Runners-Up Prizes: Goodie bag including RSPCA soft toys, lunchbox and flask

SOFT TOYS

These fantastic soft toys were kindly donated by Aurora World Ltd. The Woodlands Collection is made up of a super-cuddly rabbit, squirrel, fox and bear.

Quiz Questions

Answer these quick questions to enter the competition. Don't forget to answer the tie-breaker question too!

Tick the boxes, then fill in your name and address details. Ask your parent/guardian to sign below, cut along the dotted line and send your entry to the address shown.

If you don't want to cut the entry form out of your Annual, please send a photocopy instead.

Q1: What type of dog is featured on the cover of this Annual?
- ◯ a) German Shepherd
- ◯ b) Jack Russell
- ◯ c) Great Dane

Q2: What are baby rabbits called?
- ◯ a) Puppies
- ◯ b) Cubs
- ◯ c) Kittens

Q3: What is a badger's home called?
- ◯ a) Sett
- ◯ b) Nest
- ◯ c) Dray

Tie-breaker (maximum of 25 words):
If you were an animal what type of animal would you be and why?

....

....

Please complete the following information:

Name: _____ Age: _____

Address: _____

_____ Postcode: _____

Parent/guardian's signature: _____

Send the entry form to: RSPCA Competition, Scholastic Children's Books, Euston House, 24 Eversholt Street, London, NW1 1DBQ

This competition closes on 31st March 2013.

LUNCHBOXES

Liven up your lunch with these great RSPCA lunchboxes and flasks, donated by Vogue International. There are two designs – a tarantula and a pony.

Before sending in your entry, please read the full competition terms and conditions on page 62

GOOD LUCK!

RSPCA Fundraising

The RSPCA is a charity organisation, which means it relies on donations of money to fund all its important animal welfare work. If you're under 16 and want to help out, here are a few ways that you can get involved!

These animal-tastic cupcakes, decorated to look like cats, sheep and lions, are another great idea for making delicious food to sell for fundraising.

Fundraising Ideas

Here are some great fund-raising ideas you can take part in:

At School:

- Pupils and teachers could pay £1 to go to school dressed as their favourite animal.
- Sell any unwanted toys or gadgets to other pupils during a lunchbreak and donate the proceeds to us.
- Make animal-themed biscuits or cakes and sell them – check out the owl cookies recipe on page 47.
- Organise a sponsored event like a sponsored silence or walk.

At Home:

- Make things like greetings cards or bracelets and sell them to friends and family.
- Grow sunflowers or tomato plants and sell them.
- Give up chocolate for a week and ask your mum or dad to donate the cost of the chocolate to us.
- Have a garden or garage sale of all the toys you no longer play with.
- Face-paint your friends and family and donate the proceeds to the RSPCA.

Grrrr! Face-painting is a good way to raise money – and being a scary tiger is great fun too!

Make Owl Cookies!

WARNING: Before you start, ask an adult to help you with the oven - it needs to be set to a heat of 160°C, or Gas Mark 3.

You will need...

Plain flour (250 grams), caster sugar (75 grams), unsalted butter (175 grams).

1. Grease a baking tray by spreading a small piece of butter all over it with a piece of greaseproof paper.
2. Mix the flour and sugar together in a large bowl. Cut the butter into pieces and rub it into the mixture until it forms a smooth ball of dough.

Tip: if your hands are really warm, try holding them under cold water to cool them down. Dry them thoroughly before handling the mixture again.

3. Sprinkle flour on your work surface and a rolling pin and roll the dough out until it is about one centimetre thick.
4. Trace the owl template on to greaseproof paper and cut round the line you have drawn.
5. Place the owl on your dough and cut around the edge with a dinner knife. Repeat until the dough is covered in owls. Place them on the baking tray.
6. Use the dinner knife to make 'owly' marks, such as feathers and eyes, in the dough.
7. Bake for 20 to 25 minutes, or until golden brown.
8. Ask an adult to help you take the cookies out of the oven and transfer them to a wire rack to cool.

Use this template as the pattern for your owl cookies. You'll have a hoot making them!

How the money you raise can help...

£5 could provide a tasty dinner for a cat, dog, rabbits or other animals we rescue that are waiting for a new home.

£10 could provide bed and breakfast for an animal too.

£25 could pay for a full health check for one of the donkeys that live at the RSPCA's Lockwood Donkey Centre in Surrey.

£35 could help us purchase a pair of 'Jimmy Shoofs', special breathable medicated bandages for the hooves of rescued cows.

£150 could help us care for a wild seal until it is ready to be released back into the wild.

Going Underground

Some animals spend a large part of their lives below the ground. An underground home protects them from predators – other animals hunting them for food – and helps them to keep warm in the winter and cool in the summer.

Moles and badgers are two of Britain's most interesting burrowing animals. Let's find out more about these shy, underground dwellers...

Clever Claws

A mole's paw has a special part that looks like a second thumb! It grows after the mole is born, probably to help the little animal dig, or burrow. Moles use their claws like spades to dig themselves a network of tunnels.

Mole Facts

- Many people think that moles are rodents, like rats or mice, but moles are actually closely related to hedgehogs and shrews.
- Moles are not actually blind – they just have very tiny eyes like pinholes. Their eyes are sensitive to light.
- Each mole lives in its own network of tunnels, separate from other moles.
- Moles are insectivores, meaning that they are specially adapted for eating insects – they move up and down their tunnels, munching on any worms, slugs or insect larvae they come across.
- During autumn and winter, moles make stores of worms to eat later. As many as 470 worms have been found in one store.
- A mole can eat more than half its body weight in a day, and must eat every few hours to survive.

Messy Moles

Many gardeners in Britain consider moles to be a pest. This is because moles sometimes make a mess of their lawns by digging upwards, leaving messy molehills behind. However, gardeners in Ireland have no reason to dislike the little burrowers – there are no moles on the Emerald Isle!

Badger facts

- Badgers live in groups of about six in underground homes called setts. The setts are often very ancient as they are usually passed down from one generation of badgers to the next.
- Like humans, badger are omnivores, which means that they eat everything. Although earthworms are a particular favourite, they will also eat other insects, fruit, cereal and small animals.
- Badgers mainly come out at night when they forage for food. They have a good sense of smell and great hearing.
- It is thought that the stripes on a badger's face could be a warning to other animals – watch out for these strong jaws and sharp teeth!

In spring, badgers can sometimes be seen gathering bluebells to take back to their setts to make sweet-smelling, comfortable bedding.

Wriggly earthworms are a badger's favourite snack!

A fully grown badger is about 75 cm long – roughly the size of a spaniel.

It's a Vet's Life!

As any cat or dog knows, a vet is a special doctor just for animals. The RSPCA's vets have to deal with lots of different poorly animals, from dogs and cats to hedgehogs and foxes. Thousands of animals are treated every year, and they try to make sure that as many animals are taken care of as possible – whether they're people's pets, or sick and injured wild animals. It takes lots of hard work to become a vet, but each day is so rewarding. Just see what can happen in one day!

Seb Prior is a veterinary surgeon who works at RSPCA Harmsworth Animal Hospital in London. He loves his job, and is always very busy!

8.30am: Mungo the Jack Russell

First thing in the morning, and our first patient of the day has already arrived! Mungo hasn't been able to eat his dinner because of a sore tooth. He'll need a small operation to remove his tooth.

9am: Bandit's check-up

Accident-prone Bandit the cat gets into a lot of scrapes, so her owner has brought her in to make sure her injuries are healing well. Everything looks fine for Bandit ... this time!

10.30am: Fox in trouble

A Red Fox cub has been brought in for treatment. He was found near a country lane and has some nasty cuts after being hit by a motorbike. The team clean up his wounds and examine him. He will have to stay at the nearby wildlife centre, where he will be looked after by the RSPCA staff.

11am: Surgery for Winston!

Uh oh! Winston the German Shepherd has had an accident at the park and broken his leg. He needs surgery to fix it. We'll give him a blood test first, to make sure he'll cope with the anaesthetic, then give him an injection to make him unconscious for the operation. His leg will be set in its proper position in a cast – just like when a person breaks a bone.

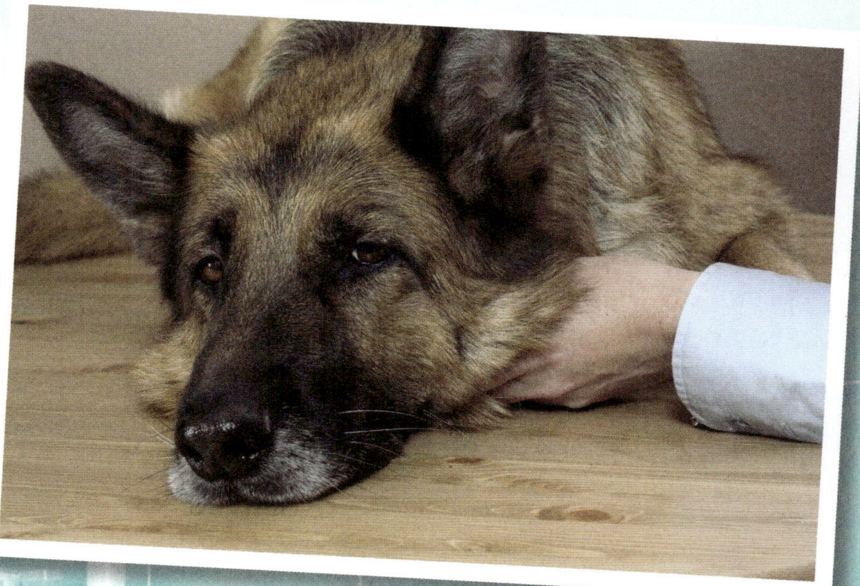

2.30pm: Checking up on Mungo...

Mungo has coped well with the operation to take his tooth out. He'll need to eat soft food for a few days, but after his gum is healed, he'll be back to his old self. He can go home today!

4pm: Rascal's X-ray

Rascal the cat has had some problems with her back before, so her owner has brought her in for a routine X-ray. Everything looks OK!

5pm: Wildlife Emergency!

A member of the public has brought in a poorly hedgehog they found in their back garden. They were worried that it had been hurt by another animal. Fortunately, our prickly little friend is just very hungry and thirsty. We'll take good care of him until he's well enough to go back to the wild.

6pm: Time to go home!

All the animals that are well enough to leave are collected by their owners and taken home to be looked after.

So you want to be a vet?

It's never too soon to start planning. You'll need to work hard at maths and science and when you're old enough, think about helping out at a local animal centre or vet's surgery – the extra experience will really help you decide whether this is the career for you.

In the Winter

Winter is an exciting time of the year, but it can be very cold, too. Pets and wildlife may need some special attention to keep them safe and warm until the spring.

Fox Food
Foxes are very hardy animals. Food may be in shorter supply during winter, but they can usually find enough to survive the colder months.

Bird Care
If you have a bird bath, remember to check the surface is free of ice regularly, so that the birds can still drink.

Seasonal Top Tips

Make Yummy Bird Treats!

Ask an adult to help you with this recipe.

When the ground is frozen, birds can find it hard to find worms and insects to eat. The fat in these bird treats will help our feathered friends keep up their energy levels and stay warm in the coldest weather.

All you need is a packet of lard, a mixture of oats and birdseed, and biscuit or cake crumbs. About 500 grams is enough. You'll also need eight or nine small yogurt pots with a 50 centimetre length of string threaded through the bottom of each one.

Ask an adult to melt the lard in a large saucepan, then stir in the dry ingredients until all the fat is soaked up. Let the mixture cool a little and scoop it into the yogurt pots, leaving the string poking up through the middle. Leave it to cool thoroughly then turn out the treats and tie them in the trees for the birds to discover.

Home for Hedgehogs
If you're lucky enough to have hedgehogs in your garden, why not encourage them to stay with a special wooden hedgehog house? They can use it for shelter and may even hibernate in it through the cold winter months.

Keep Walking!
It might be chilly, but dogs still need plenty of exercise to stay happy and healthy. Fit your pet with a reflective collar and dress yourself in high-visibility reflective clothing to make yourself visible to drivers if you're walking your dog in the dark.

In the Summer

When the weather gets warmer, it's time to keep an eye on your pets! It's also important to spare a thought for the problems Britain's wildlife may face in the summer months.

Wild about summer

You've taken care of your pets and made sure they're happy in hot weather, but what about all the wildlife that comes into our parks and gardens? Here are some handy hints for helping wildlife during the summer:

- Look out for well-hidden small animals such as frogs or hedgehogs when you are mowing or strimming the lawn.
- Regularly clean and refill birdbaths and top up ponds.
- If you have a pond make sure any animals that might fall in – like hedgehogs – have a way of climbing out.
- Make sure netting protecting ponds, or fruit and vegetables is pulled tight. Animals such as hedgehogs, snakes, frogs and birds can get caught and trapped if the netting is loose.
- Leave bowls of clean water in your garden for wild animals, such as squirrels and foxes, to drink from.

HOT FACTS

Keeping your cool is hot work when the temperature rises – whether you're a cat, a dog, a rabbit or a goldfish. There are some simple things you can do to make sure your pet doesn't suffer.

- It's very important to make sure that animals have constant access to fresh drinking water – they may need to drink more in the summer to avoid dehydrating. Remember to refill water bottles and bowls with fresh water regularly.

- Keep animals that live in cages or tanks out of direct sunlight. They should have access to cool shady areas at all times.

- Some pets can get sunburn, just like humans, so remember to protect them, especially if they have lighter skin or pale fur. Speak to your vet for advice on pet-safe sunscreen.

- Never leave a pet in a car in hot or warm weather – even with the windows left slightly open, the heat can be unbearable and can result in death. Dogs can't keep cool by sweating like humans do. They only have a few sweat glands – mainly in their feet – and have to pant to keep from over-heating.

- Animals can also overheat if they exercise too much in hot temperatures. It's better to walk dogs in the early morning or later in the evening when it is cooler than in the middle of the day.

- If your dog does overheat try to cool them down slowly by spraying them with cool, but not icy cold, water. Overheating can be very dangerous for pets, so seek urgent advice from a vet if you are worried.

Back off Badgers!

Lucky badgers were saved when the Welsh Government announced that they had decided not to kill badgers in Wales, as part of measures to control the deadly disease bovine tuberculosis. Instead, badgers will be humanely trapped and vaccinated. Sadly, the UK Government are still in favour of culling badgers so we're working hard to convince them to follow in Wales' footsteps and opt for the humane alternative for England. You can find out how to help at www.rspca.org.uk/backoffbadgers.

RSPCA Campaigns

Every year the RSPCA is busy campaigning for the better treatment of animals, whether they are farm animals, pets or wildlife. A campaign is an organised plan to lobby politicians and raise people's awareness about an issue to get their support. RSPCA campaigns often use advertisements, website content, newspaper articles, and TV and radio interviews in their campaigns to help animals. Here is a round-up of our most recent campaigns and some current ones too!

Get Puppy Smart!

If you would like a puppy, check out the animation at www.getpuppysmart.com. It offers loads of useful advice and tips about what to look for when choosing a new pet dog. It will help you think about the right dog for your lifestyle, where to buy the puppy from, how much it will cost and lots more. Time spent researching the right puppy for you really will make all the difference.

Cage-free eggs

If you love a boiled egg for your tea or enjoy eating cakes, make sure the eggs you use are from cage-free hens. Watch our Hettie the Hen animation and listen to Hettie as she explains why cage-free eggs from happy, healthy hens are the best. Look for Hettie at www.rspca.org.uk/eggs

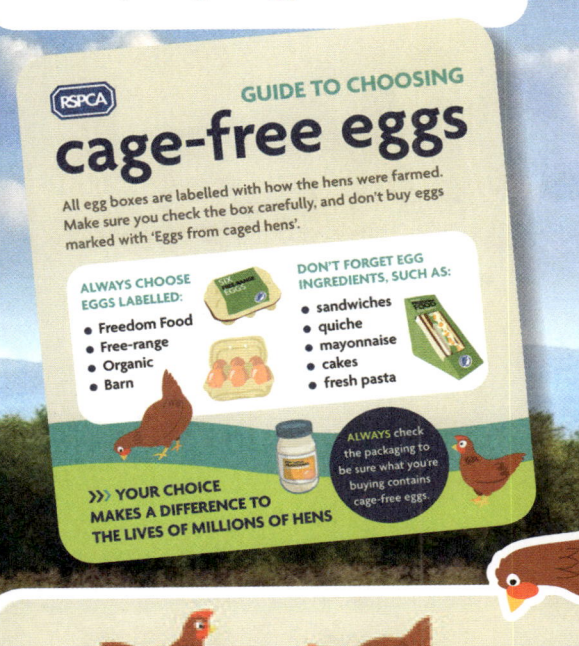

Follow the checklist:
1. Is it Freedom Food?
2. Is it outdoor reared, outdoor bred, free-range or organic?
3. Has your supermarket signed up to the new labelling code? Check here: www.rspca.org.uk/freedomfood/wheretobuy

Food Labelling

If you like roast chicken and bangers and mash, then ask whoever does the food shopping to check the labels on your food. Labels are an important way of ensuring that you can make an informed choice about what you eat. Our labelling campaign asks for compulsory labelling on animal products as we recognise that people should know how the food they eat has been farmed.

Every time we shop for food we have the power to make a difference, so if you eat meat, poultry, dairy, eggs or salmon look for the Freedom Food logo — you can be sure that the animals have been reared on farms inspected to RSPCA standards.

A Hopping Good Tail!

We joined forces with other animal welfare organisations to be part of Rabbit Awareness Week to highlight how best to look after a pet rabbit. Currently the third most popular pet in the UK after cats and dogs, rabbits are a big commitment and need a lot of looking after. Learn more about owning a pet rabbit at www.rspca.org.uk/rabbit

Join the Club!

If you love animals you'll love our Club! Keep learning about animals and having fun by joining the RSPCA's *animal action* Club. You'll get our fab magazine *animal action* six times a year and a welcome pack when you join.

RSPCA animal action

Did you know?
Dolphins only let half of their brain sleep at once!

All about *animal action*

Our magazine is full of animal news, fun facts and ways to get involved! Look at some of what's inside:

- ❉ Fun and games ❉ Creature feature
- ❉ Competitions ❉ Pets pics ❉ Fame at last
- ❉ Fab animal facts ❉ Action for animals
- ❉ And meet Dougal – the editor's gorgeous dog!

56

Fab 'welcome' pack

When you join our club you'll get all of these through your letterbox:

✻ *animal action* folder
✻ puzzle book
✻ four cute postcards
✻ membership card
✻ RSPCA badge
✻ year planner
✻ stickers

Sign me up!

If you're bursting to get your hands on all of this great stuff here's what to do. Ask an adult to go to www.rspca.org.uk/theclub and sign you up online. Or they can call 0300 123 0324 quoting AASA12. It costs £15 for one year (£22 if you live outside the UK). We look forward to welcoming you to our club!

If you like reading about animals, you'll love this fantastic new fiction from Scholastic! Each book tells an exciting story based on a real-life RSPCA animal rescue.

Wildlife: Little Lost Hedgehog

Grace finds a tiny, hungry hedgehog all alone in the flower bed. Will the RSPCA be able to nurse it back to health?

Pets: Puppy Gets Stuck

Emily's new puppy has fallen into an old mineshaft. It's a race against time as the RSPCA try to rescue him!

Farm: Lamb All Alone

Ben's home is threatened by rising flood-waters. Will the RSPCA be able to save a little lamb trapped at the end of his garden?

Available wherever books are sold from early 2013

Did you know?
Bees sometimes communicate with other bees by dancing.

Did you know?
Tigers have striped skin, not just striped fur.

Did you know?
A group of jellyfish is called a 'smack'!

Are You an Animal Expert?

So you think you know everything about Britain's amazing animals? Well, now's your chance to find out with our brain-busting quiz! You can check out the animal-tastic answers on page 61 – no cheating!

1 What is the hairy layer that covers a deer's antlers called?
a) Skin
b) Velvet
c) Coat
d) Ruff

2 How many whiskers does a cat have?
a) 100
b) 350
c) 150
d) 24

3 What is the most common bird of prey found in Britain?
a) Eagle
b) Kite
c) Kestrel
d) Goshawk

4 Which is the heaviest breed of dog?
a) Old English Mastiff
b) German Shepherd
c) Labrador
d) Irish Wolf Hound

5 What is another name for a guinea pig?
a) A South American hamster
b) A cavy
c) A fur hog
d) A mini-pig

6 What is a group of moles called?
a) A litter
b) A murder
c) A labour
d) A coven

7 When a hedgehog loses its baby spines and replaces them with adult spines, the process is called:
a) Spineing
b) Quilling
c) Spiking
d) Blading

8 What colour are the legs of a Kingfisher bird?
a) Black
b) Pink
c) Purple
d) Orange

9 What is the name for the nest of twigs that squirrels build in trees?
a) Sett
b) Basket
c) Drey
d) Twiggle

10 What is the smallest species of deer found wild in the British Isles?
a) Muntjac
b) Fallow
c) Red Deer
d) Roe

11 Which of these four snakes is native to the British Isles?
a) Cobra
b) Adder
c) Anaconda
d) Taipan

12 Which animal has the longest life span?
a) Elephant
b) Human
c) Parrot
d) Giant tortoise

13 Where do hares make their homes?
a) Like rabbits, they make underground burrows
b) A dip in the ground, often in long grass, called a scrape
c) Under hedges
d) In nests made of twigs at the bottom of small trees

14 Badgers love to snack on earthworms – how many can they eat in a day?
a) 200 per day
b) 400 per day
c) 100 per hour
d) 300 per day

15 Which is the smallest of these British animals?
a) Field mouse
b) Squirrel
c) Pygmy shrew
d) Mole

16 Where does an otter live?
a) An earth
b) A holt
c) A nest
d) A burrow

17 The green woodpecker's call is known as a...
a) Yodel
b) Warble
c) Yaffle
d) Burble

18 Which of these fully grown hunting birds is the smallest?
a) Eagle
b) Osprey
c) Goshawk
d) Kestrel

19 Which of the following is the odd one out?
a) Wagtail
b) Red Admiral
c) Red Kite
d) Green Woodpecker

20 Which animal has the worst eyesight?
a) Mole
b) Rat
c) Deer
e) Bat

How did you get on? Turn over the page for the answers.

Answer Pages

Page 16: Wordsearch

Page 17: Criss-Cross

Page 26: What Kind of Animal are You?

MOSTLY As
You're a fox – wild and clever, solitary and a bit shy!

MOSTLY Bs
You're a cat – independent and agile, fond of fish and warm places!

MOSTLY Cs
You're a rabbit – friendly and cuddly with a large appetite, you're always on the hop!

MOSTLY Ds
You're a dog – loyal and full of fun, you love running around and spending time with your family!

Page 27: Odd One Out

Picture 3 is the odd one out.

Page 27: Spot the Difference

Page 41: Animal Sudoku

A

4	2	3	1
1	3	4	2
2	4	1	3
3	1	2	4

B

9	3	4	5	1	7	2	6	8
6	7	2	3	8	4	5	9	1
1	5	8	9	6	2	7	3	4
3	9	5	2	4	8	6	1	7
8	6	1	7	3	5	9	4	2
4	2	7	6	9	1	3	8	5
5	1	9	8	2	6	4	7	3
2	8	6	4	7	3	1	5	9
7	4	3	1	5	9	8	2	6

Pages 58-59: Are You an Animal Expert?

1. b) Velvet – because it's so soft!
2. d) 24
3. c) Kestrel
4. a) Old English Mastiff
5. b) A cavy
6. c) A labour
7. b) Quilling
8. d) Orange
9. c) Drey
10. a) Muntjac
11. b) Adder – also known as a viper
12. d) Giant tortoise – the oldest one on record lived to be 177 years old
13. b) A scrape
14. a) 200 per day – that's a lot of wriggly worms!
15. c) Pygmy shrew
16. b) A holt
17. c) Yaffle
18. d) Kestrel
19. b) Red Admiral – it's a butterfly, the rest are birds
20. a) Mole

Competition Rules

Send entries to: RSPCA Competition, Scholastic Children's Books, Euston House, 24 Eversholt Street, London, NW1 1DB, unless otherwise stated.

• Entrants must be under 18 years old and must ask permission from a parent or guardian before entering • Entries are only valid if they include the correct answers and a tie-break answer and your name and address • The winner and runners-up automatically accept that the RSPCA will be using their address to notify them of their prize • One entry per competition only • The winner will be the first correct entry drawn after the closing date. The runners-up will be the next 25 entries drawn. Where there is more than one entry with all questions answered correctly, the tie-breaker will be judged. The criteria for judging the tie-breaker shall be at the sole discretion of the judges • The judges' decision is final and no correspondence will be entered into. All entries shall become the property and copyright of the RSPCA • Unless otherwise stated, all competitions are open to all RSPCA Annual 2013 readers, wherever they may live • The winner's prize includes an overnight stay at RSPCA Mallydams Wood wildlife centre in Hastings at their annual Open Wood Weekend on 27th and 28th July 2013 for a maximum of 6 family members or friends but not exceeding 6 people in total with evening meal, breakfast and lunch included • The RSPCA will contribute up to a maximum of £50 towards travel costs of the winner's group, payable to the winner's parent or guardian on receipt of evidence of travel costs • The names of the winner and runners-up may be shared with the companies and organisations with which the competition is being run for the purposes of prize delivery. Prizes are subject to availability. If in circumstances beyond our control we are unable to organise a prize, we will endeavour to organise an alternative prize of a similar value. No cash alternative will be offered • Entries must not be sent in through agents or third parties. Any such entries will be invalid • The winner and runners-up will be notified in writing within 28 days of the closing date • If an entry chosen to be a prize winner does not include valid contact details or the prize-winner does not respond within 5 working days of being contacted by the RSPCA or the prize-winner rejects the prize, the RSPCA will draw a replacement prize-winner • The RSPCA/Scholastic Ltd reserves the right to cancel the competition at any stage, if deemed necessary or if circumstances arise outside our control • Entrants will be deemed to have accepted these rules and agreed to be bound by them when entering a competition • No purchase is necessary • You can contact us in relation to this competition at Scholastic Children's Books, Euston House, 24 Eversholt Street, London, NW1 1DB • The competition closes at 12am midnight Greenwich Mean Time on 31st March 2013. No entries will be accepted after that date and no responsibility will be accepted for entries lost or damaged.

Website Addresses

If you'd like to find out more about Britain's wildlife, how to care for your pets and the latest RSPCA campaigns, check out these fact-packed pages on the RSPCA's website.

www.rspca.org.uk/allaboutanimals/pets/dogs/factfile
www.rspca.org.uk/allaboutanimals/pets/cats/factfile
www.rspca.org.uk/cats
www.rspca.org.uk/hamsters
www.rspca.org.uk/guineapigs
www.rspca.org.uk/mice
www.rspca.org.uk/allaboutanimals/pets/rabbits/factfile
www.rspca.org.uk/rabbits
www.rspca.org.uk/horsesandponies
www.rspca.org.uk/allaboutanimals/helpandadvice/seasonal
www.rspca.org.uk/dogsinhotcars
www.rspca.org.uk/allaboutanimals/wildlife/inthewild/gardenhedgehogs
www.rspca.org.uk/campaigns